## Shrews

FRONT: L 3/16"–5/16"; W 3/16"–5/16"
HIND: L 3/16"–7/16"; W 3/16"–5/16"

Tiny, delicate tracks only visible under ideal conditions.

## Voles & Lemmings

FRONT: L 1/4"–1/2"; W 1/4"–1/2"
HIND: L 1/4"–5/8"; W 1/4"–1/2"

Common around fresh vegetation. Usually walk, rather than bound.

## Harvest Mice

FRONT: L 1/4"–3/8"; W 1/4"–5/16"
HIND: L 1/4"–1/2"; W 3/16"–5/16"

The "thumb" on the hind foot is set farther back than in other mice.

## White-footed Mice

FRONT: L 1/4"–1/2"; W 5/16"–1/2"
HIND: L 1/4"–9/16"; W 5/16"–1/2"

Very common. Leaves a trail pattern like that of a miniature squirrel.

T0123836

## House Mouse

**FRONT:** L ¼"–½"; W ⁵⁄₁₆"–½"
**HIND:** L ¼"–⁹⁄₁₆"; W ⁵⁄₁₆"–½"

Common in and around buildings. Usually walks rather than bound.

## Jumping Mice

**FRONT:** L ⅜"–⅝"; W ⅜"–⅝"
**HIND:** L ½"–1⅛"; W ⅜"–¾"

Hibernates through the winter. Has extremely long, slender toes.

## Pocket Mice

**FRONT:** L ¼"–⅜"; W ¼"–⅜"
**HIND:** L ⅜"–½"; W ¼"–½"

Only four toes show clearly on the hind foot. Pads are often indistinct.

## Kangaroo Rats

**FRONT:** L ¼"–½"; W ¼"–⅜"
**HIND:** L ⅜"–1¼"; W ⅜"–¾"

Usually leaves only hind prints. Hind tracks show only four toes.

## Woodrats

**FRONT:** L ⅜"–⅞"; W ⅜"–¾"
**HIND:** L ½"–1¼"; W ½"–⅞"

More bulbous toe pads
than other small rodents.

## Norway Rat

**FRONT:** L ½"–¾"; W ½"–¾"
**HIND:** L ⅝"–1⅛"; W ⅝"–1"

Common around buildings.
Tracks are mouse-like but much larger.

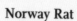

## Pocket Gophers

**FRONT:** L ¾"–1¼"; W ⅜"–⅞"
**HIND:** L ⅞"–1⅛"; W ⅜"–⅞"

Digging signs are often
conspicuous, but tracks are uncommon.

## Moles

**FRONT:** L ⅜"–⅝"; W ⅜"–⅝"
**HIND:** L ¼"–½"; W ¼"–½"

Tracks are rarely seen.
Digging signs are quite obvious.

## Ground Squirrels
**FRONT:** L ¾"–1⅜"; W ⅜"–1"
**HIND:** L ¾"–1½"; W ⅝"–1⅜"

Front tracks have prominent claws. Hibernates for much of the year.

## Chipmunks
**FRONT:** L ½"–⅞"; W ⅜"–¾"
**HIND:** L ½"–1"; W ½"–⅞"

Tracks and trails similar to those of tree squirrels, but smaller.

## Southern Flying Squirrel
**FRONT:** L ⅜"–¾"; W ⅜"–¾"
**HIND:** L ½"–1⅜"; W ⅜"–⅞"

Feet are heavily furred. Usually hops rather than bounds.

## Northern Flying Squirrel
**FRONT:** L ½"–1"; W ½"–¾"
**HIND:** L 1¼"–1¾"; W ⅝"–⅞"

Front feet usually land wide apart, creating a "boxy" track pattern.

## Red Squirrel

**FRONT:** L ⅞"–1¼"; W ½"–1"
**HIND:** L 1"–2"; W ¾"–1¼"

The smallest tree squirrels in our region.

## Eastern Gray Squirrel

**FRONT:** L 1"–1⅝"; W ½"–1¼"
**HIND:** L 1"–2½"; W ⅞"–1½"

Distinctive squirrel trail pattern. Trails begin and end at trees.

## Eastern Fox Squirrel

**FRONT:** L 1¼"–1¾"; W ¾"–1½"
**HIND:** L 1½"–2¾"; W 1"–1¾"

Our largest tree squirrel. Expanding its range but rare in cities.

## Black-tailed Prairie Dog

**FRONT:** L 1"–1½"; W ⅞"–1⅜"
**HIND:** L 1"–2"; W ⅞"–1⅜"

Live in large, unmistakable communal burrows.

## Muskrat

**FRONT:** L 1"–1½"; W 1"–1½"
**HIND:** L 1½"–2½"; W 1⅜"–2¼"

Usually found near water. Long, stout hind toes are fringed with stiff hairs.

## Woodchuck

**FRONT:** L 1⅝"–2½"; W 1⅛"–1⅞"
**HIND:** L 1⅜"–2¾"; W 1¼"–1⅞"

Large squirrel-like tracks. Typically walks rather than bounds.

## North American Porcupine

**FRONT:** L 2¼"–3¼"; W 1½"–1⅞"
**HIND:** L 2¾"–4"; W 1¼"–2"

Oval tracks with a unique "pebbly" texture. Toes rarely show.

## American Beaver

**FRONT:** L 2"–3½"; W 1½"–3"
**HIND:** L 4½"–7"; W 3"–5"

Clear hind prints are unmistakable. Trails usually lead to or from water.

## Cottontail Rabbits

**FRONT: L ⅞"–1¾"; W ⅝"–1¼"**
**HIND: L 1¼"–3¼"; W ¾"–1⅝"**

Very common. Egg-shaped tracks. Distinctive rabbit trail pattern.

## Snowshoe Hare

**FRONT: L 1¾"–3"; W 1¼"–2¼"**
**HIND: L 3"–5"; W 1½"–4½"**

Hind tracks can be much larger than front. Distinctive rabbit trail pattern.

## Black-tailed Jackrabbit

**FRONT: L 1⅝"–2½"; W 1¼"–1¾"**
**HIND: L 2"–5"; W 1¼"–2½"**

Hind heel rarely shows. Has a broader range of gaits than most other rabbits.

## White-tailed Jackrabbit

**FRONT: L 2⅛"–3¾"; W 1½"–2½"**
**HIND: L 3"–6½"; W 1½"–3"**

Hind heel rarely shows. Hind tracks are typically offset from each other.

## Eastern Spotted Skunk

**FRONT:** L 1"–1⅜"; W ¾"–1"
**HIND:** L ¾"–1¼"; W ⅝"–1⅛"

Tracks have clean, compact look. Prominent claws. Irregular gaits.

## Striped Skunk

**FRONT:** L ⅞"–1¾"; W ⅞"–1¼"
**HIND:** L 1"–1¾"; W ⅞"–1¼"

Prominent claws. Toes never splay. Trails resemble that of a miniature bear.

# Weasels

## Weasels

**FRONT:** L 5⁄16"–½"; W 5⁄16"–½"
**HIND:** L 5⁄16"–½"; W 5⁄16"–½"

Small tracks, typically in a 2x2 lope with highly variable strides.

## American Mink

**FRONT:** L 1–1¾"; W ¾"–1⅜"
**HIND:** L ¾"–1½"; W ⅞"–1⅜"

Crisper tracks than other small weasels. Usually found close to water.

## American Marten

**FRONT: L** 1½"–2¾"; **W** 1⅜"–2½"
**HIND: L** 1½"–2⅝"; **W** 1⅜"–2½"

Thick fur blurs palm and toe pads.
Trails often end at the base of a tree.

## Fisher

**FRONT: L** 2⅛"–3½"; **W** 2"–3¼"
**HIND: L** 2"–3"; **W** 1¾"–3"

Has wider trails and crisper tracks
than the American Marten.

## Northern River Otter

**FRONT: L** 2"–3"; **W** 1⅞"–3"
**HIND: L** 2¼"–3¾"; **W** 2⅛"–3½"

Usually found near water.
Trails often include slides.
May show tail drag.

## American Badger

**FRONT: L** 1⅞"–2⅝"; **W** 1½"–2¾"
**HIND: L** 1½"–2½"; **W** 1¼"–2¼"

Walks with toes turned
in. Long claws leave
prominent marks.

### Virginia Opossum

**FRONT:** L 1¼"–2⅛"; W 1½"–2¼"
**HIND:** L 1½"–2½"; W 1½"–2⅝"

Front track has starlike shape.
Hind track resembles a human hand.

### Northern Raccoon

**FRONT:** L 1¾"–2¾"; W 1½"–2¾"
**HIND:** L 2"–2¾"; W 1½"–2¾"

Distinctive 2x2 walking gait. Tracks
often resemble human handprints.

### Black Bear

**FRONT:** L 3½"–6"; W 3½"–5½"
**HIND:** L 5"–8"; W 3½"–5¾"

Five toes and robust palm
pads. Very large. Clear prints are
unmistakable.

### Nine-banded Armadillo

**FRONT:** L 1½"–2"; W 1"–1¾"
**HIND:** L 2"–3"; W 1½"–2¼"

Tracks have a distinctive
birdlike appearance.

## Swift Fox

**FRONT:** L 1"–1½"; W 1"–1½"
**HIND:** L 1"–1½"; W ⅞"–1¼"

Smallest wild canine track in the Midwest. Hind palm may not register.

## Gray Fox

**FRONT:** L 1¼"–1¾"; W 1¼"–1¾"
**HIND:** L 1⅛"–1¾"; W 1"–1⅝"

Claws may not show. Trails may begin or end at the base of a tree.

## Red Fox

**FRONT:** L 1¾"–2½"; W 1½"–2⅛"
**HIND:** L 1½"–2½"; W 1¼"–1⅞"

Heavy fur often makes pads less distinct than those of other canines.

## Coyotes

**FRONT:** L 2"–3"; W 1½"–2¾"
**HIND:** L 2"–3"; W 1⅜"–2¼"

Tracks usually narrower than in other canines. Hind palm may not register.

## Gray Wolf

**FRONT:** L 3¼"–4½"; W 2¾"–4"
**HIND:** L 3"–4¼"; W 2½"–3¾"

Strong toes may pull soil into a dome between the pads. Very large tracks.

## House Cat
**FRONT:** L 1"–1⅝"; **W** 1"–1¾"
**HIND:** L 1⅛"–1⅝"; **W** ⅞"–1⅝"

Tracks are round with a large palm pad. Claws rarely show.

## Bobcat
**FRONT:** L 1½"–2½"; **W** 1½"–2½"
**HIND:** L 1½"–2½"; **W** 1¼"–2¼"

Asymmetrical front track may be wider than it is long. Large palm pads.

## Lynx
**FRONT:** L 2¾"–4"; **W** 2⅝"–4½"
**HIND:** L 2¾"–4"; **W** 2½"–4¼"

Heavily furred feet often make pads look small and indistinct.

## Cougar
**FRONT:** L 2¾"–4"; **W** 2¾"–4½"
**HIND:** L 2¾"–4"; **W** 2½"–4¼"

Large palm pad. The largest track in our region that doesn't show claws.

## Pronghorn

**FRONT:** L 2⅛"–3¼"; W 1½"–2⅜"
**HIND:** L 2⅛"–3"; W 1½"–2⅛"

Narrow heart-shaped track. Center of the track is often slightly raised.

## White-tailed Deer

**FRONT:** L 2"–3½"; W 1⅜"–2¾"
**HIND:** L 1⅞"–3¼"; W 1½"–2½"

Extremely abundant. Distinctive and familiar heart-shaped track.

## Mule Deer

**FRONT:** L 2"–3½"; W 1¾"–2¾"
**HIND:** L 1⅞"–3¼"; W 1½"–2½"

Nearly identical to White-tailed Deer. Use habitat and range to distinguish tracks.

## Elk

**FRONT:** L 3¼"–4¾"; W 2¾"–4¼"
**HIND:** L 2⅞"–4¼"; W 2⅜"–3¾"

Large tracks are rounder than those of other members of the deer family.

## Moose

**FRONT:** L 4½"–7"; W 3¾"–5¾"
**HIND:** L 4¼"–6½"; W 3½"–5"

Enormous heart-shaped tracks are unmistakable.

## Bison

**FRONT:** L 4½"–6½"; W 4½"–6½"
**HIND:** L 4"–6"; W 4"–6"

Enormous round hoof prints can only be mistaken for tracks of domestic cattle.

# Individual Track Identification

When looking at individual prints, identify both the front and hind tracks of the animal, if possible. Once you do, these four steps can help you identify the track:

1. Study the overall shape of the track
2. Count the number of toes
3. Look for claws
4. Measure the size of the track

## STEP 1. STUDY THE OVERALL SHAPE OF THE TRACK

Is the track circular, oval or lopsided? Is it wider at the front or wider at the back? Are the toes symmetrically or asymmetrically arranged?

## STEP 2. COUNT THE NUMBER OF TOES

Be careful—there are a lot of things that can confound this seemingly simple task. One or more toes may not register clearly, or toes may be set far off to the side. Stray marks on the ground may look like toes. Try to find a couple of prints from the same foot to verify your count.

## STEP 3. LOOK FOR CLAWS

Some animals, like dogs and skunks, nearly always show claw marks. Others rarely do. While not foolproof, presence or absence of claws is a useful clue for identification.

## STEP 4. MEASURE THE SIZE OF THE TRACK

Measure the track's length and width. While animal foot sizes can vary tremendously within a species, track size will help you narrow down the possibilities.

## HOW TO MEASURE TRACKS

Measure tracks along their longest and widest points. Measure length from the rear edge of the rearmost palm or heel pad to the front edge of the foremost toe pad. The measurements in this guide do not include claws unless they are indistinguishable from the toes or the toes themselves are not visible. Measure width across the widest part of the foot, including all of the toes. Note: Getting accurate measurements can be tricky. Momentum can distort the length of the track, and soft ground, sand and snow can alter track size, and uneven ground can skew shape. Look for clear tracks relatively free from distortion. If you can, measure several tracks to get an average.

# Gaits

Gaits describe the body mechanics of an animal's movement, including the order of its footfalls and how it coordinates its limbs. Each gait leaves a distinctive pattern of tracks. Most mammals in the Midwest walk on all fours. Four-legged movement is more complicated than two-legged movement and requires some special terminology. Four-legged gaits can be broadly divided into two categories: whole-body gaits and stepping gaits.

## WHOLE-BODY GAITS

In whole-body gaits, the body flexes and extends, and movement is created by the torso and legs working together. These gaits have a syncopated rhythm and produce distinctive groups of four tracks. Whole-body gaits fall into two categories: those where each foot lands independently, called lopes and gallops, and those where the hind feet land together, called hops and bounds.

**Loping and Galloping:** In both lopes and gallops, each foot moves independently as the animal flexes and extends its body. In a lope, at least one hind foot lands behind one of the front feet. In gallops, both hind feet land in front of the front feet. Lopes can be easy, gentle gaits, while gallops are usually all-out sprints. Lopes are the most common gaits for members of the weasel family.

Skunk lope

Wolf gallop

**Hopping and Bounding:** Hops and bounds are distinguished in the same way as lopes and gallops. A gait is a hop when the hind tracks are behind one front track and a bound when they are in front of the front tracks. When bounding, an animal's hind feet straddle its front feet, causing the hind tracks to register wider than in the front. Tree-climbing animals usually bound with their front feet side-by-side, while non-climbers usually place one front foot ahead of the other. Bounding is the most common gait for most small rodents and most members of the rabbit family.

Squirrel bound

Cottontail bound

## STEPPING GAITS

In stepping gaits, an animal keeps its body level and uses only its legs for locomotion. The legs move with an even rhythm and produce a line of evenly spaced pairs of tracks. Stepping gaits can be divided into walks and trots.

**Walking:** When walking, an animal moves each leg independently and always has at least one foot on the ground. Animals can place their hind feet on the ground either behind their front track (understep), on top of it (direct register) or in front of it (overstep). Raccoons use an extreme overstep, placing their hind foot next to the front track on the opposite side of the body. Walking is the most common gait for bears, raccoons, some large rodents and members of the cat and deer family.

Deer walk

Raccoon walk

**Trotting:** When an animal trots, the two legs diagonally opposite each other move at the same time, and there is a split second when then animal has all four feet off the ground. Like walks, trots can be understep, direct register, or overstep. Overstep trots generally require the animal to turn its body slightly, allowing the hind feet to pass to the side of the front feet. Trots are the most common gaits for members of the dog family, as well as some voles and shrews.

Coyote trot

Fox trot

# Photographing Tracks

- **Shoot in the Shade:** Dappled sun is difficult to expose properly; shadows can distort the shape of the track.

- **Get Close:** Your track or track group should fill your frame. Use a macro setting if possible.

- **Include a Scale:** This helps you judge track size.

- **Shoot Straight Down:** Shooting at even a slight angle can distort a track's shape and apparent size.

- **Shoot at Different Exposures:** Many built-in light meters are fooled by sand, snow and mud. Experiment with adjusting the exposure.

- **Take Lots of Pictures:** Take lots of pictures using different settings, then pick out the best to keep.

- **Take Pictures of the Trail and the Surroundings:** Your photographic record will be more useful if you include pictures of the animal's trail and the landscape that it was passing through.

- **Take Notes:** Record where and when you took a picture, as well as information about the surrounding area, for context.

# Track Group Chart

| Track Group | STEP 1: Overall Shape | STEP 2: Number of Toes | STEP 3: Claws Show? | |
|---|---|---|---|---|
| **TINY MAMMALS** | Tracks generally well under 1" | 4 or 5 (front) 5 (hind) | Yes | |
| **SQUIRRELS** | Triangular palm pad, long toes; front foot often shows 2 heel pads | 4 (front) 5 (hind) | Yes | |
| **LARGE RODENTS** | Each track in this group is distinctive | 4 (front) 5 (hind) | Yes | |
| **RABBITS** | Egg-shaped; pads usually indistinct | 4 (front) 4 (hind) | Yes, may be obscure | |
| **SKUNKS** | Compact; stubby toes rarely splay | 5 (front) 5 (hind) | Yes | |
| **WEASELS** | Toes form an arc above chevron-shaped palm pad | 5 (front) 5 (hind) | Yes | |
| **FIVE-TOED WALKERS** | Often resemble human hand or foot prints | 5 (front) 5 (hind) | Yes | |
| **ARMADILLO** | Unique birdlike tracks; outer toes rarely register | 4 (front) 5 (hind) | No | |
| **DOGS** | Oval, large triangular palm pad; claws usually show | 4 (front) 4 (hind) | Yes | |
| **CATS** | Round, very large triangular palm pad; retractable claws rarely show | 4 (front) 4 (hind) | No | |
| **UNGU-LATES** | Distinctive cloven hoof; prints often heart-shaped | 2 (front) 2 (hind) | Dewclaws | |

*Adventure Quick Guides*

# Only Midwest Mammal Tracks

Organized by group for quick
and easy identification

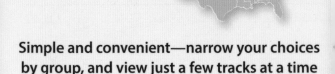

**Simple and convenient—narrow your choices
by group, and view just a few tracks at a time**

- Pocket-sized format—easier than laminated foldouts
- Realistic track illustrations with size information
- Step-by-step guide to track identification
- Track information chart and sample gait patterns
- Based on Jonathan Poppele's popular field guide

Improve your tracking skills with
the field guide and playing cards

ISBN 978-1-59193-478-3    **$9.95**

**PUBLICATIONS**
**Adventure**
an imprint of Adventure**KEEN**

**NATURE/ANIMALS/
MIDWEST**

9 781591 934783